www.finishinglinepress.com

Remnants

poems by

Ruth Derrick

Finishing Line Press
Georgetown, Kentucky

Remnants

I dedicate these poems to three who have gone before me:
my husband, Joe Derrick,
and my parents,
Gorden and Eleanor Williams—
their lives touch each verse

ACKNOWLEDGMENTS

Thanks to my children and their spouses for their support and encouragement.
Thanks to Theresa Burriss for the gentle pressure that pushed this work forward.
Thanks to my creative writing groups who gave priceless feedback.

Publisher: Leah Maines

Editor: Christen Kincaid

Cover Art: Kristena Derrick

Author Photo: Debora Sullivan

Cover Design: Elizabeth Maines McCleavy

Printed in the USA on acid-free paper.
Order online: www.finishinglinepress.com
also available on amazon.com

Author inquiries and mail orders:
Finishing Line Press
P. O. Box 1626
Georgetown, Kentucky 40324
U. S. A.

Table of Contents

Their Past

I Come For the Stories

This place—
abandoned for years.
A rusty windmill
and a stout horse barn
the only remaining witnesses
to those who lived here.

The grass, lush and green
from late spring rains
bends silently in the breeze.
No sound except
the turning
of tarnished blades
and the creek
quietly gurgling.

The voices are stilled.
But I know
if I listen
I will hear,
hear the tales
of family members
long gone.

The Ride

The car sits
resting in the shade of the tree
bothering no one.

Verna asks
You wanna ride?
I can drive it,
Alton showed me.

We three girls giggled
in pre-teen excitement
and agreed
a ride would be fun.

Verna turns the starter
and the car jumps,
the clutch unhappy
with her unschooled
foot. It lurches
and lunges
and goes across the yard
            and stops.

And we three
no ride to our credit
must help push that
monstrous heavy
car back to the shade
before Alton returns.

Body Language—1918 Family Portrait

The man is seeded in you, child.
Your future
is masked by pressed white knickers,
blonde curls,
and a stiff frown—
but it's all there.

Feet to dance
  you to countless parties.
Eyes to flirt
  girls into your arms.
A mouth to drink
  your body to disease.
Hands to grasp
  cold steel
    and end it.

Cardboard Prison

He flaps his arms
and squeals.
The doe-eyed cow
gives him scant notice.

The odor of fresh hay
mixed with manure
surrounds him.

His only toy,
a red rubber ball,
escapes his chubby fingers.
A wail announces
his displeasure.

His hands slap the sides
of his enclosure
bending the edges
of the box meant
to contain him
just until the chores
are finished.

The red ball lies
silent in the trough,
        ignored by the heifer,
forgotten by the boy.

The Dare

She grasps the grill
her tiny knuckles straining white,
legs dangling from the bumper.
She'd show her brothers.

Mother sees and runs,
arms flapping, voice shouting
in silence, the terror stills
her speech.

Father waves
and smiles,
pleased his wife
comes to meet him.

And the toddler
just one furrow away from harm
as the old pick-up
bounces and jolts down
the bumpy dirt road,
its unexpected passenger
holding dear to the frame.

The driver completely
                    unaware.

No Accident

His stubby legs carried him
the length of the yard,
past peony bushes and a scrubby pine.
He snatched up the toy pickup,
a gift for his fifth birthday,
and held it high
so little brother couldn't touch.
His sibling jumped,
stretched, pleaded.
But the older child prevailed.

The younger stomped off,
then spied a large sanding file.
He wrapped his three year old fist
around the heavy tool,
and with white hot toddler anger,
flung it,
piercing his brother's skull.

A chilling wail
brought Mother running.
And as she tugged the rusty metal
from the boy's head,
fluid began to pulse,
racing down his neck,
soaking his shirt.

Mother gathered him,
seized baby brother's hand
in both anger and fear,
and hurried to find Father.

In minutes, they'd bundled
themselves into the family car
and sped off to the hospital.
The five mile trip from the farm
held a wealth of anxious thoughts
packed into an eternal ten minutes.

The act of rage did not destroy
the brothers.
The loss of spinal fluid
did not have a harmful effect
on the boy
who grew to be an honor student,
a husband, and a surveyor.
But his barber knows
the contour
of his eighty-year-old head
will never be natural.

The Game

Dad and Lloyd were ahead
as usual.
Mom and Dorie rarely won
at Euchre,
but they didn't mind.
This monthly card game
the closest thing
they had to a date.
With ten children between them
there was little time
or money
to *go out.*

The men joked,
their leisure attitude
belying their keen
sense of the cards.
Beers sat at two corners,
rarely purchased Coca-colas
opposite them.

A knock at the door
and an unexpected visitor.
Aunt Gertude walked in
and stopped short.

Gorden, you know card playing
is a sin.

The beers disappeared
under the table.

And liquor, Lord,
what kind of example
are you setting for your
children?

Well, sister,
it's just a friendly
get-together between neighbors.

And the homebrew
is little more than colored water.

Heavens, it gets worse,
just like moonshine.
Next thing
you'll be dancing.

A slight smile crossed
Dad's face.

You may be a grown man
but you are still my little brother.
I expect you at church Sunday morning.

She strode to the door.

And for goodness sake
don't be late.

—

Lloyd,
I think it's your deal.

Inheritance

My brother got Granddad's truck
when he died.
I wanted it,
asked and pleaded,
but Buster got it.
He got
Granddad's pocket knife
too.
All I got was the World War II
Purple Heart medal.
Nice to be sure, but nothing like the worn
and leathery
Granddad I knew.
If I'd got the truck,
it would still be running.
If I'd got the knife,
it would be resting solid in my pocket,
not lost to a worthless S.O.B.
in some poker game.

Closing

Sunrise over the hilltop.
Grandma and Grandpa's place.

Hot coffee on the porch
      black and strong
      just like Grandma
      always brewed.
Bundled in her old shawl
rocking away the dawn
he sighs,
aware once again
of their stamp on this house
      the smell of lemon oiled chairs
      the well seasoned frying pan
      the softness of quilts lovingly worn.

Time to go.
A last longing look,
he jabs the "for sale" sign in the yard
and turns away.

My Past

First Time

At age seven
the fabric of a new store-bought dress
had never touched my skin.
Mother's skillful hands
always crafted my wardrobe.
But my elder sibling,
a recent high school grad,
was bringing home a paycheck.
And a special Christmas outfit
for her baby sister
was too good to pass up.

The dress was a crisp cherry red.
Delicate white lace marched
in straight rows from the waist
to the Peter Pan collar.
Two bands of the same trim
encircled the bottom
and a wide sash tied in a large bow.
The gathered skirt was perfect for twirling,
and it danced merrily
on the warm air from the floor's heat duct.

I recall little else of that Christmas
save the dress.
I recited my requisite poem
at the church pageant
and sang with my off-key classmates
during our school program.
My parts in both performances
were minor.
But my joy was boundless.

Summer Feet

Our neighbors, the Klingermans, had them.
Thirteen pairs of soles
toughened to leather.
One hundred thirty toes exposed
to dirt, grass, and rocks.
Twenty-six feet impervious
to pain and discomfort.

How I resented the way
they skimmed across gravel
like weightless gazelles.
Not a wince.
Not a grimace.
Never stopping a game of tag
or halting a jump rope contest.

I tried. Every summer,
I shed my canvas sneakers
and ventured out.
The grass felt fresh and coarse.
The dirt was warm and powdery.
But the army of pebbles on the road
attacked my tender skin.
And two rusty nails
punctured my soft hide.

Today, I love the cool smoothness
of a polished wood floor.
And the welcoming comfort
of a soft rug.
But an errant stone
on the asphalt driveway
wrenches me back decades
to painful childhood moments
and Klingerman envy.

Community Gathering

Farm couples and children
gather in the cramped
one-room school
on plank benches
and folding chairs.
Some squeeze into too-small desks.
Dad often at the center
performs in a skit,
elicits laughter
with his good friend, Lloyd.
Too young to participate,
I sit on Mother's lap
or on an uncomfortable board
next to others my age.

Until one time,
one special evening,
I recall Dad's invitation
to be part of the fun.
A family with no money
wants to go to the circus.
So they walk in backwards,
and people think they are leaving.
My four-year-old frame
steps onto the low stage,
and holds my brother's hand.
I amble back
across the wooden floor,
feet skimming the smooth slats,
and become a part of family history.

It Hurts Me More

Farms must have rules.
Safety is crucial
where large machines
can gobble small children.
Our small dairy enterprise
had a busy highway
separating buildings and pastures.
Crossing the road was forbidden.
Yet the temptation was enticing,
and one day,
I looked both ways,
and stole across the asphalt
to the other side.
My father was a small speck
on the red tractor,
but his eyes were keen.
When he saw me,
he turned for home.

I scurried back across,
and like any decent child,
I hid.
Finding me was simple.
Teaching me an important lesson,
much harder,
his tears mingling with my own.

Taken

for Dad

Borrowed.
Stolen, really.
Images of you.

Me, held close in your arms.
Us, together, feeding a lamb, your gentle hand
guiding the bottle to its hungry mouth.

Box social suppers
purchased and abandoned
till you found the one
you'd spend your life
with. Your humor that left
its dimpled imprint on its listeners.
Movies missed
to avoid those sentimental tears
you easily cried.
Grandchildren longed
for but never

met. Secondhand memories
taken from the albums of others'
claimed as my own.

This One's Mine

They weren't enough,
those vague memories
floating dreamlike around
the edges of my mind.
A ride in the truck,
a visit to the mill.
I wanted more,
more than hazy impressions
of my times with you.

Mom said we spent
hours together
your last summer,
you reading, telling
stories.

Then one day, the door
cracks open.
And just as if it were
last week, I picture
us together,
sitting beneath the pine
tree in the yard at dusk
our backs scratched by
the tree's rough bark.

You teach me
the alphabet…backwards.
And every time I recite those
sing-song lines—
ZYX and WV—
you return.

Sisters

The photo shows a chubby me
with unruly blonde curls.
Cradling me,
you look older than your thirteen years.
Our mother, in the back,
often labeled grandmother.

In that early black and white,
the only things we shared
were gender
and the same blood lines.

Sixty years down the road,
the resemblance between us is strong.
Life experiences more alike
than dissimilar.
That sense of adventure,
undeniable.
A preference for wintergreen
and stale Peeps,
surprising.
Involvement in the community
striking in its overlap.

Our matriarch,
a remarkable ninety-nine,
is healthy.
Determined.
Sometimes sharp-tongued,
still her own person.

We look at her and shake our heads,
certain of our predetermined fate.
Envisioning
our future selves
marching on to become
our mother.

Our Past

Mt. Katahdin

I sat barefoot
at the water's edge.
My toes chilled
by the mountain stream.
My shoulders soaking up
July's rays.

You lay prone
on a flat rock,
languid for a time,
your chin resting on
casual fists.

Little was said
as we watched
the water hurdle
over the rocks.
Off to the side,
a pool formed,
some of the icy liquid
gained a brief respite.

You quietly observed
the hurrying creek,
the tranquil pond.
And without turning asked
Which one is your life?

Blackberries

The picnic was planned.
The blackberries were a surprise.
Our fingers stained and wounded,
our taste buds anticipating the future pie.

The rain descended quickly,
so we packed up the remnants of lunch,
and our unexpected plunder.
Our rusty bikes,
holdovers from an earlier life,
transported us homeward,
but could not speed us past the downpour.
Our feet peddling madly,
accompanied by our mirth,
the situation somehow
making us feel like children
again.

We arrived home,
invigorated by the ride.
My green gingham shirt soaked
to my skin.
Your decades old shorts
dripping from their
encounter with the raindrops.
We straggled into the apartment
with our damp cargo,
our laughter trailing behind us.

As for the pie,
it was too sour to eat.

Last Minute Trip

The gas crisis of '79.
Risky to go more than half a tank from home.
So our spontaneous decision
to travel
brought with it an air of danger
and excitement.

Like teenagers sneaking
off to a secret rendezvous,
we packed the Camero
and trekked to Busch Gardens.

Initial stop—the Loch Ness Monster.
Your first roller coaster ride
quickly became your second
as we hurried
to experience the rush of the thirteen story drop
once again.

We had a treasure chest of experiences that day.
A lunch of brats at the beer garden
followed—unwisely—by a ride
on the Octopus.
The Ompah Band, dancing and playing
for appreciative crowds.
The Big Bad Wolf shaking our brains
till our heads pounded.
And that close-the-park-out
final ride on the "Monster"
seated in the front car.

But the seminal moment
came at the train.
We waited at the stop,
an expensive ice cream cone
in my hand.
As the engine approached
I said, *Help me with this.*
And you inhaled every bit
of my rich, creamy delight.

I stood there,
dumbfounded
and hungry.

I never let you forget it.
and thirty years later,
I still smile
at the look on your face.

Guilt

Our first race together.
You could have run faster,
much faster.
But you kept my pace.

For almost ten miles,
up and down the hills
along the streets of Annapolis,
arms pumping,
breathing labored,
muscles filling with lactic acid.

At last, we enter the stadium
and hear our names
announced.
Once around the track
to the finish line.
At the final moment,
you surge forward
so your finish time
eclipses mine.

And your remorse
over that small, selfish act
was never assuaged.
You carried it
like an annoying pebble in your shoe
for the rest of your life

Christmas Eve Morning 2000

My heart is full
as our family
stands before 1000 people
to sing together.
On stage
we pick up mics
and assume our positions.
The piano begins
as we open with the chorus.
"We who were walking in darkness
have seen a great Light."
Our bodies rock slowly with the melody
as we sing the refrain.

Both sons solo
and all join the chorus.
You drop your mic.
I pick it up
and place it in your hand.

As we resume the refrain
color drains from your face,
skin turns a deathly gray.
I abandon my spot,
and rush toward you
breaking your fall.
As you crumple to the floor
music and worship abruptly halt.
No need to shout for
the doctor in the house
for several quickly emerge.
By the time they arrive,
your eyes are open
and you've rejoined the conscious.
The words of the song
envelope you unexpectedly.
Darkness has leveled its first volley.

Regret

End of a long day.
A nighttime routine
that was never quick.
The lengthy list of requirements,
both for your health
and for your comfort,
always exceeded my expected timeline.

And when you were finally settled
splints positioned,
boots placed,
ten pillows strategically located,
a final prayer spoken,
I was spent.
My tears barely restrained
till I reached the adjacent room.
My sobs muffled so you wouldn't hear.
The emotional and physical fatigue
overwhelmed my body,
I let down,
and I wept.

To protect you,
guard your heart
from the grief we already shared,
I stayed apart
till my emotions steadied.
And by the time I retired,
you were long consumed by slumber.

I missed the spooning,
your warmth against my back,
our hands intertwined
as we drifted
to our separate dream worlds.

If I had a re-do,
I'd risk the pain I might inflict,
gather myself to your side
and take back those lost moments.

Unexpected

Speech left.
Safe eating left.
Walking solo left.
But laughter never left.
Your body shook with a good joke
or a little flatulence.

One last bit of amusement
came at my expense.
While seating you
on the commode,
nature cut loose,
and warm yellow
flowed over my hand.

Your shoulders heaved.
As my frustration grew,
your mirth increased.
The more I protested,
the harder your body trembled.
Your glee at my annoyance—
aggravating then,
treasured now.

Final Question

You were so *by the book.*
Even though novels
and non-fiction texts
spelled out the details,
you were tight-lipped.
A faithful officer,
you would never disclose
the truth of the maneuvers
of your fast attack submarine.
I joked from time to time,
I'll ask you on your death bed.

When that day arrived,
the Navy and The Cold War
were far from my conscious thoughts.
Yet from some recess,
the question emerged—
Did you ever shadow a Soviet sub?
You had no words.
You could not speak.
But your subtle nod
gave me my answer—
a *yes* I'd been certain of for decades.

If I could return to that moment,
I would not ask,
would bury the urge,
would remove that mercenary question
from our last day together.

My Now

Closing Remarks

I often say his "I quit"
was his last gift to us.
But in truth,
I expect his final gift
was far more.
As he lay in bed
contemplating the life
that awaited him,
I believe
he was praying,
doing the only thing left to him
in his diminished capacity.
Yet something valuable,
something to be treasured,
to be lauded—
lifting his family up
and committing us
to His faithful care.

Jesus while suffering greatly—
pain incomprehensible;
breathing labored;
death imminent—
took time to provide
for His earthly mother.

My husband—no Jesus—
but a righteous man
had no voice.
Yet I'm certain
he delivered us
to the Father's gentle,
loving hands.

"I Fell In Love With Your Husband At His Funeral"

…she said.

Unusual
to connect with a man
who is already gone.

My husband's funeral
was a short biography
of an ordinary man
who lived the life
God gave him.

He was accomplished.
Musically gifted,
athletically strong,
mentally keen.
And yet, those things
did not engender
a new love.

His face,
silly in its antics,
warm in its love of family,
earnest in its pursuits.
These could certainly
demonstrate the soul
of a man.

But I think it was the stories.
Stories of his fun-loving
nature.
Stories of his care and concern
for family,
right to the end.
Stories of faith,
and trust,
and surrender
to a God
Who knew
when *his* story
was complete.

The Wait

You wanted to see birds
outside the window,
view their feathery splendor
as you sat for protracted times
eating your breakfast
gazing out the window
at the distant mountains.

So your father
built a house,
erected it within your purview,
supplied the seed.

And the birds came,
large greedy types,
gobbling up the sunflower and the milo,
the millet and the flax.
Their color monotonous,
their personalities rancorous.

But you wanted color,
beautiful hues,
yellow and blue.
So I suspended a narrow cylinder
of thistle seed,
and we watched daily.
But none appeared.

Then life took a turn,
and death invited itself in.
And the thistle and the search
for beauty were forgotten
            for a time.

But my eyes were rewarded
with a glorious yellow finch,
a tiny bird of immense pigment,
who came to dine,
the day after your funeral.

Lourdes in My Bathroom

You didn't walk away on strong legs.
You didn't leave with full breath.
You didn't speak a final word on your departure.
You were not able to discard the implements
that made life more livable.
Unlike the pilgrims to Lourdes,
you needed those helpers
till the very end.
Needed the stability and underpinning
those items provided
for a body that had betrayed
you.

But the day after your passing,
as I walked into our bathroom,
my bathroom,
I saw them silently
standing in unison.
The wheel chair. The walkers. The cane.
Abandoned
by one who no longer required their services.
Just as hopefuls
who traveled to that grotto in France,
and left behind useless
crutches and walking sticks and rickety chairs,
you were cured, mended, made whole.

Two in One

We were like an egg,
you and I.
A complete item
with distinct traits.

You, the transparent white,
possessed an uncommon decency
evident to all.
I, the viscous yolk,
quietly stubborn and solid.

We lived together,
individuals yet one whole,
until God cracked the shell,
and dropped us into
His heavenly separator,
and you squeezed through
to another life.

The Sweater

I can't part with it.
Its history consoles me.
A garment smoothed
by many wearings
and washings.
The deep green faded,
the cloth supple in my hands.
The image often present
in my recollections of you.

So it hangs,
a sentinel.
Your other clothes are gone.
Your shirts long donated.
Your coats protecting others.
Your uniforms mothballed.

Some days,
I gather its softness,
drape it around me,
inhale its musky spice—
warmed by its memory of you.

Phantom Pain

The throbbing ankle
when there's only a stub
at the knee.
The aching wrist
on a ghost hand
at the end of a shortened arm.
Amputees know this pain.
I do too.

You took a chunk of my heart
when you left.
To be sure
the bleeding was stanched
by words of comfort and hope.
Stitches mended the wound
as people wove themselves
into my grief.
The scar, barely visible
because of the Great Physician's skill,
indicates healing.

Yet, when my emotional barometer
dips low,
the pain returns,
fearsome, intense
and real.

Dictionary

Recently, I went looking
for a synonym for alone.
I didn't expect to find the word
widowed.
When I turned the tables,
and checked the thesaurus
for widowed,
I found

nothing.

No
word to describe the depth
of grief,
the ache
of loss,
the lack
of you.

Life Cycle

Four poems in one

Waves pounding the shore

      balance

            the turquoise numbers pulsing his heartbeat

Current teeming with vigor

      gives

            contrast to the ebbing of his mortal frame

Never still, ever speaking

      truth

            while his voice is silenced

Vibrant cerulean water

      counters

            eyes once bright with mischief

Breakers racing to the sand

      waning

            vision now dimmed by ruthless loss

Tides' relentless motion

      life

            marching toward a knowable end